TELLING OUR STORIES

An Anthology of Faith

Volume II

PHYLLIS BYRD JENKINS

Copyright © 2022 Phyllis Byrd Jenkins
phyllisjenkins.com
Powerful Journey Anthology Volume II
Powerful Journey Publishing
ISBN: 979-83566220-2-1

Cover by: Jackie Castle
Edited and Formatted by Paula Peckham

Table of Contents

FOREWORD

Out of despair comes hope. Despair can descend through life-threatening illness, death of loved ones, unfair business practices, domestic violence, poverty, divorce – the list in this collection of stories is expansive.

As a photographer of authentic portraits and a seeker of Wise Women, I found these stories inspiring. I think you will, too.

Phyllis and I met when she invited me onto her podcast, "PowerLift Stories." She and her listeners were introduced to the women in my book, *Women of Wisdom: Honoring Grace Beauty of Strength.* I was honored to be asked to write a foreword for this collection of Wise Women stories.

Phyllis has used her God-Assignment to equip and encourage women of all ages to tell their personal, dramatic stories of how their faith in God and His word have brought them out of the darkness of despair and into the light of hope.

Although each of the women in this collection have relied on their faith, you do not need to be a Christian to be touched and inspired by their stories. They are also everyday women who have overcome challenges with strength and grace. You may begin to think differently about your personal experience. You may begin to find hope. With that hope, you may begin to move forward out of your darkness into light.

As a seeker of Wise Women, I've found that Phyllis, and all of the women she has inspired to write their stories, will make a lasting impression. May they inspire you to write your story.

Donna Edman
Award-Winning Photographer and Author

I

NTRODUCTION

Everyone has overcome something. Regardless of age or life stage. That means everyone has a story. My God assignment and my mission is equipping women to tell their stories.

Not only is it my God assignment and mission, but it has also become my passion. Whether the women write their books, participate in an anthology such as this one, speak on stage at the Powerful Journey Women's Conferences, or are interviewed on the PowerLift Stories Podcast … they are telling their stories.

Many of these courageous women tell their stories publicly for the first time. This is no easy task. Why? Because many of them are stirring up and reliving past hurts, shame, anger, bitterness, doubt, worry, and other negative emotions that kept them bound. However, they pushed through because they are now victorious and want to help others become champions of their past.

In November 2021, I took a faith walk and launched the *Telling Our Stories Anthology Volume I*. Fourteen women shared Storm Stories that had been turned into See-What-God-Has-Done Stories. The book was a great success, impacting lives across the globe. The stories brought revelation, inspiration, and transformation to their readers and sold 1001 books within sixteen days of release.

Why am I telling you this? Because I believe someone reading this book is holding back from moving forward with the assignment God has given you. If indeed that person is you, I challenge you to say YES to the assignment and watch God work through you like never before.

As you read each story, notice how it mirrors your own. But don't stop there. Look for where God is leading you to get started and to keep going. If He is leading you to tell your story to bring hope to others, reach out to me. *The Telling Our Stories Anthology Volume III* will be released next year.

513 Years of Wisdom is the powerful second half of this anthology. We filled this half of the book with wisdom from women ages 76 to 99 years old. Five-hundred-thirteen is the sum of their years. We salute and honor all these amazing women for their willingness to share their life experiences—the good and the bad. They are indeed over-comers and want to help others live a life of victory. May each of us receive their advice and learn from their lifelong lessons.

Your story matters.

Phyllis

Hear the powerful voices as the women describe their stories.

My Story

Several years ago, I heard these words: "Mrs. Jenkins, you are lucky to be alive." The pulmonary specialist who stood by my bedside in the hospital continued. "My patient in the other room has the same illness, but the blood clots have now traveled to her brain. She is not going to make it."

After a five-day stay in the hospital, I walked out thanking God for healing me of the pulmonary embolisms (blood clots in both my lungs.) I returned home and began to ponder the question, "God, You took her but left me here. What more do you have for me to do? What's my God assignment?" It was urgent that I discover the answers to these questions and move forward to live my life purpose.

I vowed not to waste time, nor allow procrastination, distractions, other people, or even myself to rob me of my God-given assignment and the reason He saved my life.

After days, weeks, and even months of soul searching, praying, and spending quiet time with God, my true purpose and God assignment was revealed in the form of the Powerful Journey Organization (empowering women to tell their stories and write their books). However, I had to approach this assignment with a different mindset than other projects in the past. In the past, I would start and stop, start and stop, and not fully commit to finishing what I started.

But this time, things were different. After all, I had just experienced a life-changing illness. I discovered the missing link to finishing my projects was **follow through.** I lacked the most important strategy for completing any project or assignment. Anyone can start something, but only a few will finish. Statistics show that 91% of people do not finish what they start.

I now invite you to pause and self-reflect. What do you need to finish? Is it the idea of starting your own business, writing a book, hosting a podcast, finishing school, painting the kitchen, reorganizing your closet, or…? You fill in the blank. It's TIME for you to recommit, start over, follow through, and finish your assignment.

One of the most rewarding feelings in the world is to know you are fulfilling your God assignment. Since launching the Powerful Journey organization, thousands of people across the globe have been blessed and moved to action by the women (and men) who have told their stories in our anthologies, annual women's conferences, the PowerLift Stories Podcast, and by those who have written their books. Annual educational scholarships have been awarded to single moms of special needs children and to graduating high school seniors.

What if I had not followed through with the assignment God had given me?

You are not reading this story by accident! I encourage you NOW to stand- up, step out, and move forward to take action with a renewed determination. The world needs what you have to offer.

Life Lessons from My Grandma

Have you ever had life lessons from your grandma? Well, that is what this story is all about.

"Momma! Momma, you overslept for church." I woke to the sound of my aunt gently waking my grandmother for church. I had spent the night in her room, sleeping on her sofa by the window.

"Momma! Momma!" My aunt's voice changed. She rushed back down the hall, the flip-flop sound of her slippers fading off into the distance. A sinking feeling sat uncomfortably in my stomach. Grandma had passed. I refused to open my eyes. The morning sun warmed me, and I thought about what we had just shared, talking and laughing the night before while watching one of John Wayne's movies.

My aunt called me, and I opened my eyes. The sun shining through the window illuminated the room. With tears flowing down my cheeks, I gazed at Grandma's baby blue church hat hanging on the corner of the dresser mirror. I stopped beside her bed on my way from the room. She slept peacefully. My aunt took me by the hand. I was twelve years old.

Memories flashed back to the times when we talked together. A feeling of disbelief came over me. As I look back, I savor those moments in my heart. I thought about never taking anyone in life for granted, and I'm thankful to God for allowing her to share her pearls of wisdom.

I was six years old in the winter of 1972. I stepped off a Greyhound bus with my mother and Marvin on a snowy day. We moved from Birmingham, Alabama, to live in New York with my grandmother, aunts, and cousins in a large three-bedroom apartment in Harlem. My upbringing took place in Harlem and Brooklyn, the neighborhood on 111th Street and 8th Avenue, known as the Ghetto. I grew up around gangs, drug addicts, and prostitution. Yet, I spent time outside, jumped Double Dutch with my friends, and played handball, Simon Says, and Freeze tag in the park. While living here, my grandmother significantly influenced me; she was loving, caring, protective, and ruled with an iron hand. When Grandma told me to do something, I did it or faced the consequences. At breakfast, she told all of us at the table that no one went out to play until we had eaten all the oatmeal in our bowls. I still hear her voice in my mind to this day.

My grandmother was also born in Birmingham, Alabama, a young widow raising seven children through the Jim Crow era and didn't have any modern-day conveniences. Some people called Grandma "Mattie P." P stood for her middle name, Pearl. She had a stringent and robust personality, and she never gossiped. She would always say, "If you don't have anything nice to say, don't say anything." She was very observant and always knew when something was wrong with us. Grandma sacrificed and endured raising her siblings after her mother passed when she was young. She went through a lot but knew only God carried her through those challenging times in her life.

One of the many great lessons I learned about my grandmother is to listen to what she told me. One day, Grandma told us to stay near the stoop so we wouldn't get into trouble. I sneaked and went with a group of kids to the super park. I convinced my cousins we could join them. Unbeknownst to us, Grandma was sitting on the park bench with a lady. She jumped up and pulled us out of the group. She said, "Didn't I tell you to stay by the stoop?" My cousins all pointed the finger at me, saying I told them it was okay to go. Grandma lined us up by the bathroom, and each of us received our whipping for being disobedient. She said, "There are two roads in life: a right one and a wrong one. Make sure you choose the right one." I thought sneaking off was right; we all would have fun and not be bored sitting on the stoop. I was oblivious to the crimes in my neighborhood infested with drug addicts hooked on heroin and gangs hanging out in the park smoking marijuana. This scripture reminds me always to listen. *The way of fools seems right to them, but the wise listen to advice.* Proverbs 12:15 NIV

One day when I was nine years old, the teacher left the classroom to get a box of blackboard chalk. A girl named Jeanette and some classmates always bullied and picked on a girl called Sabrina, and she would always cry. They kicked her chair, knocked down her books, and called her derogatory names. Sabrina ran to the girls' restroom. I followed Jeanette and her buddies to one of the bathroom stalls. Jeanette told the girls to kick the door in, and one by one, they all began kicking the door. I followed, kicked her door, and ran. The girls raced away, laughing and yelling obscenities. Then I stopped running. Something inside me made me think about my grandmother's words: do unto others as you would like them to do unto you.

Jeanette was my friend who lived in my apartment building. We jumped Double Dutch every day and sat on the stoop playing jacks. This lesson from my grandmother came in on so many levels; it made me stop and think about how I would feel if someone bullied me all the time. I would hate the constant harassment. I felt bad after kicking Sabrina's door in. What we did was wrong.

I thought about Grandma warning me not to hang around the wrong people to and watch the company I kept. And I thought about how I would feel if I was treated this way. So I stopped being friends with Jeanette and started a new friendship with Sabrina. Jeanette got into trouble, fighting during the school year.

This lesson profoundly impacted my character. From then on, I always treated others with respect and kindness and surrounded myself with like-minded people. The Bible reminds us to beware of the company we keep. The scripture says, "*Do not be misled: Bad company corrupts good character.*" 1 Corinthians 15:33 (NIV)

On a cold Saturday morning, I played with Marvin and my cousins, taking turns flipping on the mats in our hallway. Then Grandma called me to her room. She pointed at her chair. I walked over and sat down. "Tomorrow, we are going to church. I want you to start learning about the Lord." Grandma explained the importance of prayer and having God in my life. She told us to say our prayers at night and always to pray. I was so captivated, leaning forward, listening to every word. "You are a good girl. Never change who you are and never stop learning. Life can be tough, but always work hard and do your best. I had to work hard in my life, but God carried me through some tough times." Grandma told me how challenging it was raising her siblings while taking care of her debilitated mother as a teenager. And after her mother's passing, she sacrificed her future so they could go to school and have a better life. Raising her younger sister and brothers became a life-changing event, where her role switched to being a mother. Her words intrigued me, and I absorbed everything she said. Sometimes I understood, and some things she shared I couldn't understand. I learned this precious lesson from Grandma about love: we are willing to give anything to ensure our loved ones are safe.

The next day, we all went to church, and I enjoyed the Sunday school lesson on Noah and the Ark. The story about God saving Noah, his family, and the animals from the great flood fascinated me. After class, I shared what I learned with Grandma while we all walked back home. I reflected on this lesson, and about the importance of prayer and having God in my life. I have always prayed, read the Bible, and kept the hunger and thirst to seek Him throughout my life. And this scripture makes it clear. *Those that seek Me early shall find me!* Proverbs 8:17 (KJV) I learned from Grandma that I'm never alone, and I continued an ongoing hunger to seek Him until adulthood.

Have you ever been scared for your life? I had an encounter I will never forget. One hot summer evening, we had all just finished seeing a double feature at the cinema in Times Square. We walked toward the subway, laughing and talking about the films. While walking along, we passed a bunch of folks standing in a crowd, looking at something. I was curious to see what they watched, so I wandered toward the crowd, getting closer and closer to the group. People chattered, and a fire truck whisked down the road with sirens fading off into the night. Someone gently pulled my hand backward; it was very subtle. I assumed it was one of my cousins, but it didn't register in my mind. I had no idea what was happening. I continue to peer into the crowd, trying to see past the tall figures blocking my view.

Then, in my spirit, a firm voice sounded amidst the crowd, traffic, and chattering. It told me to turn around and look. I obeyed the voice, looked up, and saw a tall black man beside me. The presence of this stranger shocked me. I frantically snatched my hand, and it slipped away from his grasp. I ran away so fast, my heart pounding in my chest. My cousins called to me. I yelled, "Did you see that man?" My cousin asked, "What man?" No one else saw him, and he vanished quickly.

I wouldn't be where I am today if God wasn't in my life. He's the reason I'm here to tell you this story. Whenever you are in a challenging situation or afraid, remember this scripture. *Fear not, for I am with you: be not dismayed, for I am your God; I will strengthen you, I will help you, I will uphold you with my righteous right hand.* Isaiah 41:10 (NKJV)

You can trust His promises in your dire hour. God is always right on time. I held on to Grandma's lessons into my adulthood. They gave me a burning desire to know Him throughout my career in the military. While stationed at Yokota Air Base in Japan, I always visited the Air Force base chapels and enjoyed the sermons.

One Saturday afternoon, I went to a water park with my friends; it would be my last day at Yokota Air Base in Japan. I was delighted to get on the water slide, hugging each curve as it poured me into the pool. I jumped up, filled with enthusiasm, wanting to get on more rides. The next day, I had a piercing, excruciating pain in my left side. After seeing the doctor, I discovered I had a pinched nerve, and that relief would come soon when I arrived at my next base in England.

Upon my arrival, I met Tracey, who welcomed me to my dorm. She invited me to the base chapel, and I shared with her about the pain in my left side. I was taking Motrin, but when it wore off, the sharp pain came back.

On Monday, Tracey told me she had already told the captain, a base chaplain, about the pain I'd been experiencing. She told me to meet with him. At lunchtime, I met with Captain Campbell inside the aircraft hangar, in his trailer. He opened the Bible and read scripture about healing. Then we prayed together. Captain Campbell asked, "Do you believe?" I said yes.

Later that evening, the pain slowly intensified as the Motrin subsided. I thought about what Grandma had told me—God is always with me and always to pray. I began to pray to God about this pain and believe He would heal me. I heard a pop, and the pain was gone. I got up, thanking God for hearing my prayers and healing me. What a relief! Thank you, Jesus! The pain was gone and never returned. Have faith and trust in His promises like it says in Psalm 30:2 (NIV). *LORD my God, I called you for help, and you healed me.*

Can God bring people into your life for a reason? I'm here to tell you He does. In the fall of 1993, I separated from Dyess Air Force and settled in Dallas, Texas. I asked my Air Force buddy and roommate, Sonya Jones, a native Texan, about finding a church home. Even though we visited many churches, I continued to search. Two years later, I moved to Arlington to attend college, still searching for a church home. I thought about Grandma telling me always to pray, which I did. I asked God to help me find a church home where I could grow and learn His word.

One afternoon, I went to Office Max to type a letter for school on one of the Brother electric typewriters. I walked over to the copier machine to make a copy. The one beside me was out of service. The only available one had a lady standing over it, photocopying her textbook. I stood behind her, waiting impatiently. I asked, "Are you going to make all those copies?"

What a pleasant surprise. The woman's name was Sherry, and we began talking about school and the Lord. She asked me whether I had a church home. When she learned I did not, she invited me to her house and shared with me about the Bible and getting baptized.

Later, I studied in the book of Peter. He tells the house of Israel that God has made Jesus, who was crucified and resurrected as both Lord and Christ. I read Acts 2:37-38 (NKJV). *Now when they heard this, they were cut to the heart, and said to Peter and the rest of the apostles, Men, and brethren, what shall we do? Then Peter said to them, 'Repent, and let every one of you be baptized in the name of Jesus Christ for the remission of sins, and you shall receive the gift of the Holy Spirit.'* I thanked Jesus for answering my prayers. The following Sunday, I went down the aisle, got baptized, and began my journey as a new convert.

One night while lying in bed, I heard His voice. "Finally, you come to Me." I will never forget Jesus wrapping His loving arms around me and showing me an abundance of love and peace.

I share this lesson because my grandmother profoundly impacted my life and led me to Christ. My grandmother could not read, yet she had the knowledge and wisdom to instill in me the importance of having God in my life. I learned to always seek the Lord in everything I do. I carried this into my adulthood and never lost my faith. I stepped out on faith for the military. As a result, I joined the Air Force, despite failing the Armed Services Vocational Aptitude Battery (ASVAB). I was persistent in studying and practicing the test with a recruiter until I passed the exam. I'm thankful for the opportunity to travel to different countries and settle in Texas. I enjoy volunteering. Being a Big Sister to three Little Sisters was very rewarding. One of them is currently in college. I'm active in my church. Being in the prison ministry is a great way to be involved in God's work. In 2018, I completed my master's degree and walked across the stage with my mother. I retired from a municipality and am currently working for a federal agency. I learned to trust God and realized He was always with me and guiding my path.

As for you, reader, do you know your purpose in life? In the Bible, it says, *For I know the plans I have for you," declares the Lord, "plans to prosper you and not to harm you, plans to give you hope and a future.* Jeremiah 29:11 (NIV) I encourage you to reflect on the following lessons:

- You will have a lot of noise to distract you; remember to listen to wise advice and always stop and think before you act.
- Be mindful of the company you keep and ask yourself, "Are they being fruitful in my life?"
- Are you setting aside some time in your day to pray? The Bible says, *Do not be anxious about anything, but in every situation, by prayer and petition, with thanksgiving, present your requests to God.* Philippians 4:6 (NIV)

Do you think God brings people into your life for a reason? Have you ever prayed to God to find a church home? Have you accepted Christ? I searched with questions on my mind and prayed for a church home. I believe there are no coincidences regarding the people God places in our lives. I know God answered my prayers on that sunny afternoon at Office Max. Sherry Brown and I established a friendship, and we sat down and had Bible study, which led me to baptism, a church home, and a growing relationship with my Lord and Savior. When you seek the Lord, He will come to you, just like He came to me. God arranges these relationships for us. He often puts us in the path of others to be the friend that shows them not just God, but also how to have a personal relationship with Him.

As for you, reader, it is no coincidence that you are reading this. If you are searching and have questions, please feel free to reach out to me at vdarbonne272@yahoo.com. I would love to hear from you. And always remember! Jesus loves you! He waits for you to come to Him; throughout life's failures or struggles, you can trust Him! In Proverbs 3:5-6 (NKJV), *Trust the Lord with all your heart, and lean not on your own understanding; In all your ways acknowledge Him, And He shall direct your paths.* And most of all, savor the moments in your life. I savored the seeds of lessons my grandmother planted in my life. Thank you for reading my story. Always remember your life is precious. We each carry a special gift from God; never take it for granted. You are special, and God has a purpose for you.

About Me

Vicki Darbonne is a Christian and a faithful servant for Christ. Known as Vicki Lynn Escott, she was born in Birmingham, Alabama, and raised in Harlem and Brooklyn, New York. She is an Air Force Veteran who served overseas and continued in Air National Guard and Air Force Reserves.

Vicki enjoys serving in various areas at her church, including teaching a second-grade Bible class and in a prison ministry. She is passionate about sharing her faith with family and friends.

She holds a bachelor's in general studies from Texas Christian University and a master's degree in business administration from Amberton University. Vicki is a retiree of the City of Plano and currently works for a federal agency. She is an avid reader, loves traveling, volunteering, cooking, and enjoys reading with her book club and journaling. Her favorite scripture is Proverbs 3:5-6 (NKJV). *Trust in the Lord with all your heart, And lean not on your own understanding; In all your ways acknowledge Him, And He shall your direct your paths.*

Pushed Into Purpose

In November 2021, I worked in a local government municipality as a team leader. On Tuesday, November 16, while performing my daily routines, I received a phone call from the city manager. He asked me to come to his office.

As I entered his office, he asked me to shut the door and have a seat. The human resource director was there, seated to my left. She intentionally avoided making eye contact with me.

The city manager proceeded with the reason he called me into his office. He told me there were two complaints coming out of my department (the Municipal Court) against me as the Court Administrator. He also stated, "Normally I would have just called you in to discuss the complaints, but I feel it needs to be investigated by a third party." At this point, I was not told what the allegations against me were, only the alleged violations of two city policies. The single question the city manager asked me was, "Who is your go-to person while you are out of the office?"

He advised me he was placing me on a one-week administrative leave pending an investigation. They then released me immediately. I walked back to my office accompanied by the human resource director.

As I collected my personal belongings, the human resource director stood in silence. She said to me on the way out, "The city manager will be in contact with you within a week's time. It will not take long." I spoke with my staff and advised them I would be out of the office for a week.

On my drive home, it suddenly came to me how swiftly things, people, positions, and places can change. However, I did not realize this would be the day my life would shift in a new direction and that a fresh and amazing experience with the Lord would begin.

The next day I reflected on the meeting in the city manager's office, and it seemed as if I had been exiled from the people I saw and worked with every day. He instructed me to not have any contact with those in my department or any other city employees during this period of investigation.

Amazingly enough, I didn't play the role of a victim or feel sorry for myself. God then revealed to me this was a great opportunity to dig my heels in deeper with him, return to my quality time in prayer, study the Word, and meditate on his goodness.

To prepare myself for what could happen within the coming days, I met with two employment attorneys to seek advice on my unprecedented situation. In all my years of working and interacting with many types of people, this was a terrain I've never navigated. I had never been investigated and treated like someone who had no morals or values.

Two days later, Human Resources contacted me, advising me a meeting was scheduled with the investigator on the upcoming Friday. It was on this day God began to encourage me to continue to focus my mind on his Word through scripture in Philippians.

Whatever is true, whatever is honorable and worthy of respect, whatever is right and confirmed by God's word, whatever is pure and wholesome, whatever is lovely and brings peace, whatever is admirable and of good repute: if there is any excellence, if there is anything worthy of praise, think continually on these things [center your mind on them, and implant them in your heart]. Philippians 4:8 (AMP)

He spoke prophetically in my ears: "You will no longer give of yourself to individuals who hate, despise, abhor what I have deposited within you." Matthew 7:6 (AMP) "Your season has shifted, and I am bringing you into a new realm of Glory."

Think about it. Do you recall a time in which someone falsely accused you, or you experienced an unfair situation you knew was not handled properly? Conducted by individuals who had evil intentions and felt ill-will toward you? Or perhaps these individuals despised you or were intimidated by your courage to stand in truth, without compromise of ethical, moral, and honest core values?

Did you have people in your life who supported you through the process? Especially when those with whom you sat in leadership trainings, workshops, and meeting rooms treated you as an outcast, as one who had committed a horrific crime! Oh, the lies and deceit, not to mention the manipulation constructed to destroy your name, character, and everything you worked to build!

Say with me: **"I AM VALUABLE AND ACCEPTED BY THOSE WHO HAVE THE CAPACITY FOR MY PRESENCE."**

As you reflect on times you were treated unfairly, how did this make you feel? And how did you come through this process? Did you have support? The vital things that got me through this challenging situation were:

- Deepening my prayer life and relationship with the Lord
- Support and encouragement of my family and friends
- Positive self-talk & faith affirmations

As Friday (*the day of my testimony*) fast approached, anxiety, worry, and uncertainty worked to disturb my peace. To maintain, I refused to give way, and stood my ground in faith; trusting and believing my heavenly Father would carry me through this trial. On the day of testimony, I entered the police department doors with anticipation and confidence, ready to voice the truth in contrast to any false allegations against me. During the two-hour questioning with Rob, (the third-party investigator), I was asked a series of questions regarding the allegations Human Resources had presented to him. As I listened, it was quite clear and easy to identify the individuals who had been previously questioned by the investigator. Mind you, most of them no longer worked for the city. There was no doubt an evil plot and conspiracy to remove me from the position of Municipal Court Administrator.

The interview finally ended after two long hours. The investigator stated his report would most likely be submitted to the city the following week, and for me to expect a decision the Monday after the Thanksgiving holiday.

After **twelve** long days, on Wednesday, December 1st, 2021, the city's human resource director called to inform me the city manager wanted to meet with me the following Monday. By this time, my faith was secured in the one who I knew to hold the future.

Listen, you must take courage in the fact—God always goes ahead of you and will reveal His plans as you keep moving. To no surprise, during this period of waiting, I dreamed of a meeting with the city manager sitting in the conference room as I walked in. When I entered the room, I carefully observed my surroundings, where he was seated, and the environment. He then told me to have a seat. I calmly positioned myself directly across the table from him, and he proceeded to say, "I have made a decision." At the same time, he slid a document in front of me to read. It stated the city had decided to terminate my employment.

I immediately awoke from the dream and knew the Father was preparing me for the outcome and the final decision of the city manager. Therefore, my state of mind and spirit were prepared for what I was about to face.

Please understand during the trial of your faith and the testing of your character, the Lord will never leave you hopeless! He so lovingly encouraged my heart in the Word of life every single step of the way.

It is my sincere prayer that your heart, mind, and soul be filled as you take comfort in these scriptures that guided, strengthened, comforted, and lifted me during my lowest moments.

The Lord is my shepherd [to feed, to guide to shield me], I shall not want. Psalm 23:1 (AMP)

Finally, brothers, whatever is true, whatever is honorable, whatever is right, whatever is pure, whatever is lovely, whatever is admirable—if anything is excellent or praiseworthy— think on these things. Philippians 4:8 (Berean Study Bible)

But I say unto you, love your enemies, bless them that curse you, do good to them that hate you, and pray for them which despitefully use you, and persecute you; Matthew 5:44 (KJV)

[25]*I once was young and now am old, yet never have I seen the righteous abandoned or their children begging for bread.* [26]*They are ever generous and quick to lend, and their children are a blessing.* [27]*Turn away from evil and do good, so that you will abide forever.* [28]*For the Lord loves justice and will not forsake His saints. They are preserved forever, but the offspring of the wicked will be cut off.* [29]*The righteous will inherit the land and dwell in it forever.* [30]*The mouth of the righteous man utters wisdom, and his tongue speaks justice.*

31The law of his God is in his heart; his steps do not falter. 32Though the wicked lie in wait for the righteous, and seek to slay them, 33the Lord will not leave them in their power or let them be condemned under judgment. 34Wait for the Lord and keep his way, and He will raise you up to inherit the land. When the wicked are cut off, you will see it. 35I have seen a wicked, ruthless man flourishing like a well-rooted native tree, 36Yet he passed away and was no more; though I searched, he could not be found. 37Consider the blameless and observe the upright, for posterity awaits the man of peace. 38But the transgressors will all be destroyed; the future of the wicked will be cut off. 39The salvation the righteous is from the Lord; He is their stronghold in time of trouble. 40The Lord helps and delivers them; He rescues and saves them from the wicked, because they take refuge in Him. Psalm 37:25-40 (Berean Study Bible)

Twelve days after the investigation, I arrived at City Hall for the final meeting with the city manager. As I entered his office, there sat Kathy, the human resource director, to my left, as cold and callous as I remembered from before. Some would say it was ironic that the scheduling of the meeting took twelve days,. But nothing our Father allows to happen is a coincidence, but instead is used for a divine purpose.

In my research and studies of the number twelve, I learned it represents authority, governmental rule, and completion. As God's Kingdom representatives, we must understand we operate from a higher realm and have the legal power to legislate and make decrees here in the earth by the Word of God, who is the final authority! Job 22:28; Luke 10:19 (AMP)

I proclaim to you this day: "ACCEPT WHAT GOD ALLOWS."

The hour-long meeting concluded with the city manager giving me an option to resign or be terminated. As I listened to their statements and observed their actions; there was one little thing the human resources director obviously failed to do before the meeting—her research on me.

In the strength of the Lord, I looked the city manager directly in the eyes as I countered his suggestion. "What about retirement?"

He immediately deflected the question to Kathy. She shrugged her shoulders and said in an insensitive tone, "I guess if you qualify."

The city manager then gave me two days to make my final decision on what had been discussed. In all honesty, I was hurt, disappointed, furious, and relieved—all at the same time—with so many emotions and thoughts going through my mind as I exited his office for the last time.

One of the greatest revelations I received from this entire experience was realizing when people reject you, they no longer have capacity for your greatness, as you have truly outgrown their limited thoughts and restricted boundaries. This unfair experience, which seemed so horrific, would be the very thing that would push me into my divine purpose and life's mission.

Have you ever been rejected or pushed out of a job, or any place? Let's take a closer look at what being pushed actually means. The definition of push is:

1. Move forward by using force to pass people or cause them to move aside.

2.Exert force on someone or something.

It can also be summed up as *being shoved, thrust, propelled, pressed, or forced.*

That situation, designed for you to fail and give up hope, may be the point for you to advance, and possess the promises God ordained from the beginning of time!

"You have now come to the point of no return."

In case you haven't noticed, in the world as we know it there are a number of people who lack integrity, on the job, in marriages, friendships, churches, governments, business, organizations, boards, leadership, communities and more. According to the Merriam-Webster dictionary, integrity is defined as "the quality or state of being complete or undivided."

"To thine own self be true"

~William Shakespeare~

I have learned valuable lessons over the course of my life and especially from my most recent experience in the workplace as a departmental leader. For your journey, I have provided some key insights for practical living.

1. **LIVE** authentically by remaining committed to your Christian beliefs and core values.

2. **REFUSE** to allow other people's fears, insecurities, and opinions to make you feel uncomfortable to the point you compromise the truth.

3. **PLACE** your expectations and hope <u>only</u> in God the Father. Psalm 62:5 (AMP), (MSG)

Take courage, knowing your faith will endure the fiery furnace! You will see and experience the right hand of God working all things together for your good, in your favor, and that same hand will continue to carry you as His righteousness prevails. Isaiah 41:10 (AMP)

There may come a time on your journey you experience the fiery furnace just as three Hebrew boys did who vowed to worship and honor their King by defying the status quo of the crowd, but one thing is certain. God has a rescue team to pull you out with no residue of guilt, pain, hurt, disappointment, worry, or heartache on you. Daniel 3: 8-30 (AMP)

My workplace experience is not the end of my story, but only the beginning of something new. My original goal was to retire from local government within twenty-five years. As one would have it, twenty-four years was God's chosen number. I left, only to become self-employed full-time in my own business, Unique Foundations Enterprise, LLC. I am also the first author in my family, and I obtained my state's license for Life, Health, and Accident Insurance. Always remember your future is brighter than yesterday if you submit all your dreams, plans, and visions to the creator, God Almighty.

DECLARE TODAY: I WEAR A CROWN OF VICTORY AND A CLOAK OF FAVOR!

It is my sincerest prayer the words of this story bring healing to the hurting, hope to those who have experienced disappointment, slander, and criticism, and restoration to what has been lost, stolen, and neglected.

About Me

Angelia is a woman of faith who lives by foundational core values and morals. She is self-employed as the managing member of her business, Unique Foundations Enterprise, LLC and is the co-founder of the 501-3c non-profit Life Revisions Center in San Antonio, TX. Having grown up in extreme poverty Angelia also provides financial advocacy as a licensed Health and Life insurance agent. Angelia is passionate about women's empowerment, entrepreneurship, community engagement, and serving in the Kingdom Marketplace of ministry.

"I AM resilient, courageous, and unique!"

Where Is Hope?

I search for a desire for things to happen while I walk through the pain. I look for a woman who has walked in my shoes. There are many, some in the same area as I search. One day, sitting alone in despair, I happen to turn on the television. I sit quietly, watching, taking in all their experiences. As I watch, I find myself in all three of the ladies. While I sit there, I notice we all have the same response, but nowhere to turn for help.

This I declare about the Lord: He alone is my refuge, my place of safety; he is my God, and I trust him. Psalm 91:2 (NLT)

Brokenness is when you feel all hope is gone. I wonder why this has happened to me. On the third day of court, the judge mentions I will need counseling. What I hear him say is, "You will need help!"

I respond that my children can't see me like this. I know only that I must stay happy for them.

That's when I cried and realized domestic violence caused my brokenness. Many mornings in the wee hours, I would cry silently so my children wouldn't hear. Days after court, I stayed away from home and my children because I was in a ball of tears for hours.

Turn to me and have mercy, for I am alone and in deep distress. Psalm 25:16 (NLT)

I had to make a conscious decision that I, not only for myself but for my children, had to leave. I didn't want them to get older and learn to accept abuse or become an abuser themselves. It took me four years to go through the stages of letting go.

I was a stay-at-home mom. My son attended school, and my three-year-old daughter stayed with me. One day, I stayed in bed to rest from the previous night's altercation with my husband. I was watching television. The children were out playing with friends and enjoying the beautiful day. My daughter came to my bed during her busy day of playing. She asked me important questions. The first was, "Mom, are you okay?" Then, "Mom, did Daddy do this to you?" *How did she know?* In return, I gave her answers of peace.

The final straw came when my daughter and I watched television. The last of domestic violence came out of nowhere. I spoke to my daughter while she was there, listening and watching the abuse I received. I expressed some words, ignoring the verbal and physical lashing of pain.

God spoke through her for me to let go at that moment. In my mind, I heard, "It's time." After years of living under abuse, I spoke to God, my eyes closed. *I give up! I hear you!* It was the release of myself and my children from years of pain.

First came emotionally and mentally letting go. My mind went through many stages of the pieces of letting go, and four years of building up to this decision. First, finding a job to provide for myself and my children, and giving up what I dreamed a marriage, with children, should be— questioning myself about how they would feel about what would take place. Would I be able to survive? I left home at twenty and had never lived independently. Would our new life keep my children in the same standard of style, where it wouldn't impact them emotionally or mentally?

Through the questions I asked myself, I took the Big Step! Letting God lead and direct me down an unknown journey was nothing but faith. I told God my faith was in Him, and I trusted Him! Trust was the big issue at this point in my life. My prayer scripture within my weakness is Matthew 6:9-15. My body was tired and exhausted from the trauma. I prayed those scriptures each night before bed.

We finally moved out of the home of pain. The strangest thing happened as I drove behind the U-Haul. Leaving also caused me pain. I broke into tears, wondering why. I called my mother and explained my emotions. She answered, and her words gave me the strength to not look back.

In our new home, we sat in the living room and my children began to open up about all they had seen. I realized how quiet they'd held themselves in the previous house. As I listened, I became aware of how much they'd understood at such a young age. I answered my children: "We are a team now and will get through our years of pain. No more harm can come to our lives."

The LORD is my rock, fortress, and savior; my God is my rock, in whom I find protection. He is my shield, the power that saves me, and my place of safety. Psalm 18:2 (NLT)

There were many nights I would cry silently from the pain. I would release these hurts in the wee hours. It was my time alone. My children would be asleep, with the exception of one night of comfort from my son. I was always reticent within my tears. I embarked on songs of worship and scriptures to console me in the darkness. The first scripture was Psalm 23. I would repeat it in my head until I fell asleep. I was a singer in my childhood, singing in the church choir. Songs of worship would be upon my heart in those early hours, even if I only repeated four words of the song. It was from my heart I sang in pain.

But in my distress, I cried out to the Lord; I prayed to my God for help. He heard me from his sanctuary; my cry to him reached his ears. Psalm 18:6 (NLT)

I remembered when a couple of things happened early, not too long after I was married. I called my mother, and I asked some specific questions. She didn't know why I asked during this time; I kept many things to myself.

Once we had finished our conversation, that is when I asked God why. I surely didn't understand. I have always kept a Bible beside my bed since I left home. On November 3, 2009, I went to a Christian bookstore, looking particularly for a Woman's Study Bible. Much has been said of men in the Bible. I wanted to study a little deeper to help heal myself of the trauma I faced as a woman.

I was traveling the journey of a domestic violence survivor diagnosed with PTSD and depression. Through God's grace and mercy, he showed me this verse.

Come quickly, Lord, and answer me, for my depression deepens. Could you not turn away from me, or I will die? Let me hear of your unfailing love each morning, for I trust you! Psalm 143: 7-8 (NLT)

I played "I Trust You Lord" each morning to start my day. We may be broken but are still beautiful in God's eye. I trusted him in my afflictions, the pain and suffering.

I will always praise the Lord. I will constantly speak his praises. I will boast only in the Lord; let all who are helpless take heart. Psalm 34: 1-2 (NLT).

The second and third songs of the morning were "Fragile Heart" and "Someone Watching Over Me." I was being joyful in hope.

Rejoice in our confident hope. Be patient in trouble and keep on praying. Romans 12:12 (NLT).

The fourth song of the morning was "God in Me." I have learned about faith, hope, and love.

Depression hit me hard one day; it brought fatigue and defeat. I stayed home to soak into sorrow. Whew! It was the most extended nine hours alone. I tried to sleep through it, thinking I would feel better. The next day I booked an appointment with my health provider. She told me I was battling depression. I had to pick myself up! Behind the smile of every day, hidden pain was still suppressed.

I realized I was faced with triggers, overwhelmed with frustration, anxiety, panic attacks, and anger. Yet, all silently, behind the hope and smile. I learned the meaning of Psalm 46:10.

Be still and know that I am God! (NLT)

I was blessed with many caretakers of my children. This allowed me to run to a place of peace—Myrtle Beach, South Carolina. I thought a full gas tank would get me there and back. I would find a hotel facing the ocean. Back in the day, it was very reasonable for a quick trip, Friday through Sunday. I only carried a few things along the way: a Bible, a novel, a suitcase, a two-liter Coke, and a large pizza to enjoy a lock-in alone. At first, I didn't get the outcome I sought, but it became medicine for my mind, body, and spirit. How did this all come about?

Forgiveness! Let's take a deep breath. Early in my situation, I had three dreams. The last one I ignored. Did I ask why? Yes, I asked for forgiveness.

Make allowance for each other's faults and forgive anyone who offends you. Remember, the Lord forgave you, so you must forgive others. Colossians 3:13 (NLT)

The Message version reads verses 12-14: *So, chosen by God for his new life of love, dress in the wardrobe God picked for you: compassion, kindness, humility, quiet strength, discipline. Be even-tempered, content with second place, and quick to forgive an offense. Forgive as quickly and thoroughly as the Master forgave you. And regardless of what else you put on, wear love. It's your basic, all-purpose garment. Never be without it.*

Whew! Yes, a lot to carry after domestic violence. Walking away, you feel you are taking the weight on your shoulders simply to keep a smile. I remember one who had in many of my journeys described me with my head held low. I couldn't look up because of embarrassment. When I returned to work, many approached me to ask why I didn't smile. I started to smile! I began to fill up with what the scriptures and the music I listened to said to me, finding my hope and love. Love came to me with fulfilling hope in others.

Growing up, I was blessed with a family who believed in faith, hope, and love. My father was the pastor of his church, and my mom sang songs of praise and worship. There are six siblings between us, with other adopted brothers and sisters. We all had specific duties to fulfill in the church. My main task at church was singing. Before age eighteen, God showed me faith in three incidents.

The first one was in the middle of the night, three in a row. During the first two nights of awakening, I walked into my parents' bedroom with my concerns about a dream. My mom's response was to read Psalm 91. I was always quiet but would hear many problems.

Second, when my brother deployed, our family prayed for a safe return—faith stepped in, with me placing a plate at the dinner table for him.

Third, was the birth of my son. The doctor delivered bad news. But God had already shown me my baby boy would be healthy. Faith, hope and love have helped me along my way.

During my time of walking through domestic violence and at one point overwhelmed by it, trying to commit suicide, I cried out to the Lord! I found his strength in Psalm 18:1 (KJV). *I love you, Lord; you are my strength.*

Sometimes you may feel you can't leave the situation or are stuck in it. Grab hold on to faith, keep walking, and don't look back. When you let your situation go, the Lord God will open new doors for you to walk through and lean totally on Him. After checking out so many apartments and rent homes, I thought I would never qualify or would find a place for my children and me. Or when, soon after walking away from my abusive situation, the truck that was paid off caught on fire. When we see things going wrong despite God making things suitable for us, there will be days we may feel the Lord isn't there, but He is. When those hectic days of living come upon you, you find yourself in hopelessness, pain, worry and, fatigue. Find your joy through things you love (music, singing, or decorating) or through a gift God equips you with. Set yourself free!

Last, at times, my heart was full of so much pain. Walking through my journey, here's my analogy. It was like my life was a potato with unbelievable stick pins piercing through. Letting go of past hurt is taking the pins out and allowing those holes to be filled with the love of our Lord God. We scrape each thin layer away with a peeler.

Healing from trauma doesn't come overnight. It's a process. God's word tells us we have authority and dominion on the earth. We have control and power over PTSD and depression. We have a say over our mind, body, and soul through the Lord God. Allow the Lord to walk with you daily. We are His children, and He loves us.

I am leaving you with a gift—peace of mind and heart. And the peace I give is a gift the world cannot provide. John 14:27 (NLT)

God's loyal love couldn't have run out, and his merciful love couldn't have dried up. They're created new every morning. How great your faithfulness! I'm sticking with God (I say it over and over). He's all I've got left. Lamentations 3:22-24 (MSG)

Thank God because he's good because his love never quits. Tell the world, Israel, "His love never quits." And you, the clan of Aaron, tell the world, "His love never quits." And you who fear God, join in "His love never quits." Psalm 118:1-4 (MSG)

Thank you, Yahweh, for your faith, hope, and love!

"If you find the deepest you, you will find Him."

About Me

Chasity Lewis-McMillan is a woman of faith in Christ. She's loving, persistent, and passionate. Out of six children, she is the fifth child. Blessed to be born into a family of faith and love, she's compassionate, with a heart to gather among family and friends.

Some of the titles she's worn are a veteran's wife, a preacher's kid, and a mother of three beautiful children. She loves her family dearly.

A motivator, a positive listener who is honest with her input and delivers it with love, she is a domestic violence survivor. Thankful for her family, who shared their strength and love, she courageously stayed active in the community with her children, spreading compassion and encouragement to other families.

Chasity served with dedication in the Military Health System for thirteen years.

She is tenacious with the flexibility to bounce back. The Club Pilates blog, a nationally recognized blog, featured her, telling the story about her journey to recovery from a car accident that fractured many vertebrae in her spine. She empowers many through her success story.

She's currently a mentor with Dr. Ken-Lyn Associates, a youth mentoring program and is an overseer of missions in her community. Through coaching, counseling, and empowerment, this organization brings wisdom to families in San Antonio, surrounding areas, and nationally.

Chasity is a world travel professional business owner called PlanNet Marketing. "It's the Scenery for Me" is her logo. Within her story, she loves to call her travel sceneries an "Island" where she lets go of day-to-day living. A place to rejuvenate her mind, body, and spirit.

She is a glowing light who always thinks and cares for others and strives to remain optimistic. She is willing to take significant risks and is excited to make a difference in everything she does.

Chasity has recently returned to work in a position she's passionate about. And is now an author!

Her statement: Forgive, Live, Love and Laugh!

~Insights and Reflections ~

Five Hundred Thirteen Years of Wisdom

She is clothed with strength and dignity.
Proverbs 31:25

It is with great delight I present to you the following women, ages 76 to 99 years old. These women are indeed clothed with strength and dignity. Their stories will amaze you and give you hope, inspiration, encouragement, and fuel for your journey.

The advice shared has been gained from their momentous mountain-top experiences and their deep valley trials. But each one of these courageous women recognizes the power, love, and grace of God in their life.

Lean in and get ready to learn from 513 years of wisdom.

Phyllis

Mrs. Ada Robinson
Age 82

How God Protected Me Through It All

My name is Ada Robinson. I am the firstborn of eleven offspring of Lucille and Adolph Brown, born in Helena, Arkansas. I am eighty-two years old and the mother of six children, four whom I birthed and two whom I inherited. I am the grandmother of fifteen, great-grandmother of sixteen, and great-great-grandmother of nine. I have been happily married to Michael Robinson for the past twenty-nine years.

I am the current owner and operator of The Village of Natural Teaching. I am a graduate of Barbara Brennan School of Healing. I'm qualified to be the following: a Natural Health practitioner, a certified Journey practitioner, a licensed massage technician, a Bowenwork practitioner, and a colon hydrotherapist.

I also am an ordained minister and a Spiritual Life coach. Biases and Diversity with the Brennan School of Healing is one class I teach.

I have a Bachelor of Science Degree from Northeastern Illinois University. In the past, I taught Language Arts.

I have been a social worker for the Department of Children and Family Services.

This is approximately 50% of my professional resume. To understand the true significance of this list of accolades, it's important you understand the story of my parents. Many of my lessons, my drive for success, and how I live my life came through my experiences as their daughter.

Lucille's and Adolph's Stories

My mother's name was Clara Lucille Lindsey-Brown, however, we called her Lucille. She was a twin, born first, and was named after her mom. Grandmother Clara had birthing complications the midwife could not handle. My grandfather went for help, but the doctor couldn't come quick enough. Mother's twin brother died during the birthing process, along with their mother. My grandmother Clara's siblings became angry and wanted to blame someone for the tragedy. So they held my grandfather accountable and chased him away when he returned. He never knew the other twin passed, and he was unable to connect with his daughter, my mother.

Because Mother was without either parent, my great-grandmother, Narcissi, stepped in to fill that role. She had twelve kids of her own, Clara being the youngest. My grandmother, Clara, had passed away when she was twenty-one years old, never having the opportunity to touch or hold Mother. My great-grandmother, Narcissi, passed away when Mother was ten years old.

With an absence of parental figures in her life, Mother didn't have an example of what a parent's role in a child's life should be. As a result, I missed out on the motherly nurturing and parenting that is essential for the growth and development of a child.

My father's name was Adolph Brown. He was the oldest of two boys. He had a sixth-grade education. Because he was the oldest, his dad made him quit school and work to help with the family business. His younger brother was allowed to continue his education and was not required to work. Because of the difference in treatment, Daddy developed an angry disposition that continued throughout his entire adult life.

Daddy was more of a disciplinarian than a nurturer. As a little girl, I always tried to do whatever was necessary to please him and prevent him from being angry with me. I looked for the approval and nurturing he was incapable of giving.

He was twenty-five years older than my mother and treated her as if she was his little girl instead of his wife. Eventually, as the family grew, Daddy often charged me with the responsibility of "taking care of my mom."

Ada's Story

I was born and started my education during the Jim Crowe Era. Because of this and where we lived, I could not go to school consistently. Being the oldest, I was required to look after my siblings while my parents and brothers who were old enough worked the cotton fields. I was required to cook, wash clothes, and tend to my siblings to ensure that they behaved. Daily during this time, Daddy came in from his work in the field and whupped each and every one of us, me getting the worst of it.

When I got to attend school, the other kids were far ahead of me because they had participated all year. The teacher seemed to have no interest in helping me. One day, so happy to finally be in the classroom, I attempted to read a passage out of a book. My teacher said, "Shut up and sit down, little girl. You can't read."

This comment caused me to become very introverted. I have managed to be delivered from that, but even with all the accolades listed above, to this day something inside of me freezes up when I am asked to read aloud.

When I was eleven years old, my father left us and went to Chicago in an attempt to make a better living for the family. He asked Mother to stay put until he returned for us. His goal was to make some money and find a place for us to live. He sent small amounts of money for her to buy food and pay the rent.

In hindsight, I believe he ran away from the challenges of life. With my mother being so much younger than my father, her interests and lifestyle differed greatly from his. She was never home. While I never had proof, I suspect she dabbled in extra-marital affairs. Mother went out partying every night. The money Daddy sent was not used to pay the bills.

She eventually moved us in with the aunt she grew up with, who had six children of her own. Combined, fourteen of us lived in one home. With my mother and aunt partying all the time, they left me to take care of all the children, including cooking for them. This was a challenge because flies filled my aunt's home. As I made food, I strove to cover the pot when I stirred the food so flies would not get inside. There was no way to prevent the flies from getting in the food because there were so many of them. The steam from the pot drew them. I picked them out to avoid feeding them to the children, but I refused to eat any of the food.

This was such a hard time for me because I was often sad about having the responsibility of taking care of all the children and my dad constantly instructing me to "take care of your mom." After a month or two, Mother decided to leave for Chicago. How exciting! We would ride a train and finally be with Daddy. I hoped I would no longer have to take care of my mother.

When we got to the place where Daddy lived, a man at the desk let us into his room after my mother convinced him we were supposed to be there. Daddy didn't know we were coming.

He lived in a rooming house for men. The bathroom was down the hall to the left of our room, and the kitchen was down the hall to the right. The bathroom and kitchen were community space, shared by all the other residents of the house. Sadness threatened again because we were limited to one room. The best job Daddy could get was a job as a window washer. Window washers didn't make enough money to pay rent at a place big enough for all of us, and we could not stay there because it was only for single men.

They allowed us to live there for three months until Daddy could find an apartment. Once again, he gave me the responsibility of taking care of my mother and my siblings in this new environment.

Mother was afraid to leave the house, so she made me go out and find the store. I was so scared, but I had no choice. I didn't realize it then, but that was a blessing for our family. When I got to the store and selected the items from my list, I gave the cashier a $20 bill. She gave me my change. When I counted it, I discovered she gave me $20 too much, so I gave it back to her. She was so happy she asked me, "Little girl, do you want a job?"

After checking with Mother, I started working at my new job. Daddy saved his money for an apartment, therefore we had very little food. We were accustomed to having only one meal a day, but during this time, we could not even have a full meal. My new boss, by God's grace, realize we weren't eating, and she started sending me home with expired food she couldn't sell. We lived on that so Daddy could save for our apartment.

My father never acknowledged my contribution to our family. They took the money and food as if it was my responsibility, at eleven years old, to support our family. My father found an apartment on the south side of Chicago, and we finally moved. It was in a basement with no windows and one door. It was damp, cold, and smelly. I now had to take two buses to get to work, and I was so scared of becoming lost. My fear forced me to learn the route.

Mrs. Fannie, my boss, wanted me to continue working for her after school started. She said where we lived would be too far for me to travel once I was in school. She told me to ask my parents if they were willing to move into a small apartment she had. Even better, within three months she would have a larger one come vacant that we could take. They said yes. I was so happy I could continue to hang out with someone who really appreciated me.

We lived right across the street from the Coliseum, which made Daddy happy. Even in his anger, he loved wrestling and sports. He could go across the street and attend the events.

There were many things of interest my parents went to see at the Coliseum, and children got in free, which allowed us to attend events, too.

There were many blessings for us during this time, but there were disparities as well. It was finally time to go to school and my first time being in a "real school." I had no friends or suitable clothes. I had one skirt, one blouse, one pair of shoes, and one pair of socks. No one knew what grade I was in. They placed me in a grade according to my age. I was harassed because of my southern accent and black dialect. I hadn't had a conversation with anyone other than my parents, and I had never been formally taught English grammar. I had no educational foundation.

During school, we prepared for the Christmas holiday program. This was the first time I'd had this experience. I was so happy. That is, until the teacher snapped at me, "Shut up, little girl, you can't sing. Just open your mouth, but don't let a sound come out. I will not have you messing up my song." This was so painful for me, but being a good little girl, I did as she instructed.

Despite other difficulties, I graduated from the eighth grade and then finished one-and-a-half years of high school. Due to a series of life changes and unfortunate incidents, and the fact my educators constantly told me I wasn't college material, I took a break from school.

One of the life-changing incidents that took place was the unplanned pregnancy of my firstborn, my son. I married shortly before his birth and quickly realized my new husband didn't like to work. I would have to figure out how to make a life for my family. Coming from a history of working, starting at eleven, I had already developed a drive to do what it took.

I started working at a daycare owned by black females who became my mentors and lifelong friends. My next job was in a restaurant—that position didn't last long. A patron swatted me on the rear end, and I slapped him. The owner reprimanded me, saying the customer was always right.

The next job didn't last long, either. One of my mentors taught me to sew, and I thought I'd use those skills to obtain a factory job. I was hired to sew at a hat factory. That job was worse than picking cotton—only lasted half a day! That's when I got the big wake-up call. I had to do something different if I was going to raise my children. I knew that to provide forward momentum for my children in their lives, I had to discover how to move forward in mine.

While working with a caseworker for my aging father, the idea was planted to go back to school. During our discussions about Daddy's care, the caseworker sensed the sadness in my spirit. She gave me vital information that allowed me to get the resources to return to school. By the grace of God, I enrolled in Malcolm X Community College *without* a high school transcript. I went on to receive a bachelor's degree from Northeastern Illinois University.

From there, I obtained many other positions and gained numerous certifications. None of it would have happened if the caseworker had not provided me with the information I needed to go back to school. I reached out to thank her once I got settled into Malcolm X and was told they never had an employee by that name.

Life Lessons Learned Along the Way

• We can listen from within.

• NEVER GIVE UP.

• Sometimes we must do things even when we are afraid.

• Each situation contains teachers, even when they are challenging.

• Even in genuine sadness, there is ALWAYS something to be grateful for.

About Me

Ada Robinson is an adjunct teacher for the Barbara Brennan School of Healing. She teaches classes on diversity and health-related issues. She has also been instrumental in developing programs for the school that teach students how to work positively with different ethnic groups.

In conjunction with her husband of twenty-nine years, Michael Robinson, she is the owner and operator of The Village of Natural Teaching. Ada works with clients via Zoom to aid them in formulating a healing plan for themselves, which encompasses developing a support team to aid in achieving their health goals. Other services from The Village of Natural Teaching include long-distance healings, prayer support, counseling and the growth and distribution of wheatgrass.

Ada's life mission has always been to support others in learning to be independent, self-sufficient, and to live under the will of God. Her philosophy has been that to live under the will of God, you must maintain your physical house. For this reason, Ada developed programs to support others in detox regimens, which include healing and maintaining the body through living food.

Ada resides in Marshall, Michigan on forty acres of land with her husband. She is the oldest of eleven offspring and the mother of six adult children, four that she birthed and two that she inherited. She is also the grandmother of fifteen, great grandmother of sixteen, and great-great grandmother of nine.

At the golden age of eighty-two, Ada continues to take on new adventures. Many have labeled her as the busiest senior citizen they know. She loves to read, swim, and be in the great outdoors when the weather is warm. She also enjoys connecting and pouring into teenagers and young adults, providing them with wisdom and encouragement.

Mrs. Ada Simmons
Age 76

Spirit-Led Living

I recently returned a phone call. The number belonged to a couple I knew from a church I had previously attended in North Texas. They were admired and involved in the life of the church. They both were ordained as elders, taught Sunday School, and the wife was an exceptional musician and organist for the church. I sang in the choir. Occasionally, but not recently, the wife and I would visit by phone.

It was the husband who received my return call. After extending greetings and small talk, he explained he was in the process of transferring and saving his contact directory to a new phone. He said his finger had slipped on my name, but he had no reason or intention to secure my number in his phone. What a sting! I attempted to offer a positive response. "I am so sorry this happened to you. I would never want you to be uncomfortable," I said. "Please rest assured that God has secured both of our numbers."

It never fails! Large or small, daily living has its crises. You name it. A hurtful statement can be a dark time, a very dark time.

During my childhood, teachers used corporal punishment. My twin cousin and I shared the same classroom in first grade. When she was punished, I was punished so that I would not tell my aunt, her mother.

In fifth grade, the student behind me cut my "pigtails" because he could not see. The teacher required my mother to secure my hair down on my head. How that hurt!

My siblings and I were the topics of envious conversation among our friends, as my parents were some of the few who were active in school affairs. Mom made our clothes. We didn't own a car, and our parents kept us near with mostly family activities. Talk and teasing can hurt.

Indifferent treatment can hurt. I was the fifth of six children. There were always two in college at one time. My family moved to public housing during middle school to secure more room "for my four girls," as Mom indicated. My parents often reminded us of God's love and encouraged working together to build a better life. They taught us to pray for the small talk of others. I found this difficult growing up.

During my sophomore year of college, after years of suffering from a cough that produced blood, I was forced to have a lobectomy. They removed one of my lungs. I missed my junior year and time with my peers. I thought I would never get well. I was declared disabled by the state of Alabama. It was a battle to return to Dillard University in Louisiana because of the disabled designation rendered by the state. Again, there was hurtful talk. I could not change that.

I focused on my health and changed my major to education to focus on special needs. I finished early and was hired to teach before I graduated.

As a young mother making my home in New Orleans, my health failed again. The doctors discovered I had only one kidney. My second child was premature, born after I suffered two miscarriages.

Of the six children, I was the only child to make my home in the South. My mom was diagnosed with colon cancer. I cared for my parents in every capacity from the time my children were in middle and high school until college. My mom saw only high school graduations. My dad was able to witness the college graduations. Between my oldest sister in the New York/New Jersey area and me, we made a loving, caring environment work for their desires. It was a difficult and full-time job.

After suffering through my parents' death (Dad also died in 2003), Hurricane Katrina hit with a force like no other to every family living in my subdivision in New Orleans. For six months, my husband and I were homeless. First, we lived with my oldest sister and her husband for two weeks. Then my son Jimmy and his wife, Kim, had a baby and we stayed with them in Colorado for a while to spend time with our grandchild. From there, we stayed with my daughter, Jana, in Los Angeles. Finally, we purchased a home in McKinney, Texas. McKinney has rocked my world in diverse ways. I won't kid you. During this period, I saw glimpses of the pit, but I didn't allow it to bring me completely down.

I believe God sent me a message through a dream about my dad. Alone in that empty house, no furniture, no things to surround me, I revisited my childhood. I saw me and my siblings, sitting with my dad in a circle, reading and discussing the Bible. I could hear his tenor voice singing "Amazing Grace." It woke me from my sleep. I felt like Daddy was telling me, "You're going to be okay. Just wait for God."

My birth city of Eufaula, Alabama, with the help of my brother, found me, prayed with me, sent funds, and reminded me God was in the storm and with us now.

My life of choral music provided the opportunity to give voice to God's promises of hope and comfort. I was blessed to have my daughter nearby to help me find a church home as I moved through the valley of the shadows. God had His plan, and I just needed to be obedient.

The destruction of Hurricane Katrina found me when I was settling into retirement from Orleans Parish School District. I had enjoyed ten years as the Student Teaching Coordinator at the University of New Orleans. In addition, the following organizations would assist in using my skills to support the school of New Orleans. STAIR—Start the Adventure In Reading—was highly successful in its tenth year at Claiborne Presbyterian Church in New Orleans. In that tenth year, JCPenney bestowed the Golden Rule Award for my founding and service to those failing first graders in public schools of New Orleans.

I was installed as President of the Greater New Orleans YWCA in the spring of 2005. I had an amazing spiritual and overall growing experience in gaining God's freedom for relational kindness while serving on the Presbyterian Child Advocacy Network. It was in my retirement years that my friend Sandra sponsored my induction into Alpha Kappa Alpha Sorority, Inc. My biological sisters were so delighted.

God has a way of using our circumstances to remember the counsel of who He is in our lives. My opportunities of retirement were left behind. I was in a strange city and purchased an affordable house in what I thought would be a growing community. My spirits were lifted as my daughter used her knowledge as a new employee in Dallas to assist me in the right places to purchase affordable materials to design window coverings for an empty home. My son used his vacation that summer to package the furnishing that could be saved from the hurricane damage and delivered them to our new home in Texas.

Things began to look up. Being alone in an empty house was a blessing. I meditated day and night. It was so new to be alone. I learned to talk to God, listen to His voice, reflect on the darkness of the past, and understand how all of it prepared me for the future of what God had in store for me. I accepted and understood it was necessary for my husband to settle our affairs in New Orleans. God taught me that He rescues us. Even from the financial stresses of a new home. Our purchased home in a newly established subdivision, Trinity Heights, was challenging. Energy bills were extremely high. We had not settled on our property in New Orleans and had to continue to pay HOA dues and other policies to restore that home.

What a blessing for an infrared assessment, costly but necessary. The builder, following the receipt of the infrared assessment report and the determination of the lawyers, was instructed to blow insulation into the walls and attic, seal the bricks on the entire house, install gutters, and repair the leaking part of the roof around the chimney.

God provides reliability. The regional office of the YWCA located me here in McKinney and arranged for me to work out of the YWCA in downtown Dallas. There, I met Parminder Gill (Pam), Director of Volunteers, who I later hired as a consultant in restoring the YWCA of New Orleans.

We lean on various aspects of life to get us through relationships and possessions, but the only thing that will never let us down is the true reliability of trusting God. It was a team of three, treasurer Neshelle Nogess; Pam Gill, consultant; and I. We delivered a debt-free agency, a Homeland Secure Grant, and fundraising complete from sister agencies. This package was delivered to members in New Orleans two years later, on March 1, 2007. The current Governor, Kathleen Babineaux Blano, extended an official statement acknowledging outstanding leadership as President of YWCA of Greater New Orleans and commitment and dedication to the rebirth of the agency after Hurricane Katrina.

God provides love in all spaces and all things. In joining the membership of First Presbyterian in McKinney, it was love that made it possible for me to continue my work and allowed my continued service with the Presbyterian Child Advocacy Network. First Presbyterian Church learned of Children's Sabbath with the first observance of National Children's Sabbath on October 26, 2006. When I addressed the worship committee, they were also made aware of the Decade of the Child initiative. I loved that it provided the opportunity to work with children's ministry and teach Sunday School and Vacation Bible School.

The 2008 Mission Yearbook published an article about this work with children in the McKinney area. Various other articles were written regarding work dedicated to the interest of children displaced by Hurricane Katrina.

God provides hope and confident assurance. My world, on the surface, was chaotic. The opportunity to enroll relocated survivors in middle and high schools in Destination College at the Central campus in McKinney restored hope for the future. Destination College focused on college readiness. I was more excited than the participants about Destination College. There was even more confident assurance as Dallas Area Interfaith provided training to organize the survivors. The iron rule was "Don't do for others what they can do for themselves." The Katrina Survivors Network was the work of the survivors.

We assisted families in getting housing and brought additional money into North Texas, especially for housing. We organized to get preschoolers enrolled in Head Start in Dallas. "Comfort for Kids" was a program modeled after 911 and implemented in schools to assist teachers with the educational care of post-traumatic times. Skill QUEST, modeled after the Workforce programs of the Industrial Areas Foundation, was a workforce program supported by the Dallas Area Foundation. It was managed by and became a non-profit success story of the Katrina survivors. Skill QUEST, Inc. provided second-chance college students with the opportunity to train for hard-to-fill jobs through the Community Colleges in North Texas. These students received associate degrees. The tuition, books, and career counselors were available to ensure success. Through Skill QUEST, over 100 students received training in living wage jobs with salaries of $40,000 or above. It was a sheer delight to be involved in Skill QUEST, recruiting and supporting the stability of survivors and others in the North Texas area. It was God who enabled me to be a founder of Skill QUEST, to lobby for the program each year, promote and seek potential students, serve on the Board, follow the participants for up to two years on the job, and to watch families grow secure and hear children speak of going to Mommy's and Daddy's school. Skill QUEST was a family program. It was hope.

The Library of Congress recorded the story of Skill QUEST ten years after Hurricane Katrina. Saving this story, according to the interviewer, was imperative! It was the work of a few citizens advocating for themselves and bringing about social change.

Visit storycorps.org to find out more about my story. Whether in chaos or perfect order, life is good. God suffers with the world, and God gives us bountiful hope. We must believe and know that when life hurts, there's tomorrow. You grow stronger and wiser with every bump in the road. Embrace your mistakes and learn from them. Build relationships that lift you up, and you can likewise inspire. Listen! Be guided by the Spirit. In a politicized, polarized society, let the Spirit guide your way of life to consider the common good and to demonstrate your commitment to supporting your community responsibly. Yes, help others! That is why we are here on earth! It gives you joy beyond what you can imagine! My best advice is to praise God in all things and follow the model of Psalm 30. Looking back, as I testify to God's goodness in trial and tribulation, God's favor is always greater than God's anger.

About Me

Ada T. Simmons is a retired educator with a thirty-three-year career span as a regular educator, special educator, and an assessment teacher in the public school system of New Orleans, Louisiana. She spent ten years of her career in the Department of Curriculum and Field Experience as a Coordinator of Student Teaching at the University of New Orleans. Simmons also served as a curriculum and tutorial consultant to the Urban League of Greater New Orleans. She is credited as the founder of a ten-year, award-winning tutorial program, Start the Adventure in Reading (STAIR), in conjunction with Claiborne/Peace Presbyterian Church and the Omicron Lambda Omega Chapter of Alpha Kappa Alpha Sorority.

Ada and her husband James III (Jim) have been married for fifty-five years and are the parents of two wonderful children, James IV (Jim), a chemist who resides in Broomfield, CO and Jana, a marketing executive in Los Angeles, CA. They are the proud grandparents of James V (Jimmy) and Jason.

Following Hurricane Katrina, Ada, with her husband, Jim, spent time in Jackson, MS, Broomfield, CO, and Torrance, CA. They have claimed McKinney, TX as their home for the past seventeen years.

Ada has never been a stranger to community involvement and immediately connected with YWCA of Dallas as a Trainer with Comfort for KIDS. This connection led her to Dallas Area Interfaith (DAI) through an invitation to a Red Beans and Rice dinner. That dining experience, reuniting and fellowshipping with New Orleans neighbors at Saint Elizabeth Anne Seaton Catholic Church in Plano, was the first of many training activities that prepared Ada for her work as a Leader with the Katrina Survivors Network (KSN), a member of the Coordinating Board of DAI, and Vice President, Founding Board member of Skill QUEST, Inc.

Ada's DAI training has given direction and purpose to her community involvement in McKinney. Her story and service with the KSN and DAI has been published in Presbyterian Mission Yearbook, the Presbyterian Child Advocacy Network (PCAN) newsletter and was accepted by the Library of Congress/Smithsonian in February 2015. During its 25th Anniversary Celebration, Dallas Area Interfaith highlighted the Katrina Survivors Network as one of the DAI success stories. During this 2015 celebration, the *"From Disaster to Discovery"* theme highlighted the recovery service of the Katrina Survivors Network.

Other community service includes Trinity Heights HOA Board 2007-2011, McKinney Community Block Grant Commission 2010-2011, McKinney Housing Authority Board of Commissioners, North Texas Job Corps Community Council, and Martin Luther King, Jr. Power Breakfast Committee with Collin County College District. Ada is a 32-year member of Alpha Kappa Alpha Sorority, Inc., and an active member of the Chi Zeta Omega chapter in Plano. Ada is an active member of Trinity Presbyterian Church of McKinney; an ordained Elder, currently serving on the session; Community Coordinator of Committee On Racial Equity (CORE); a Stephen Minister; and a member of the choir.

Several awards to acknowledge outstanding community service are the 1999 JC Penney Golden Rule Award, 2005 New Orleans Young Leadership Council Role Model, 2009 Alpha Kappa Alpha South Central Regional Mary Louise Williams Social Justice Award, 2013 Collin College Chancellor named and presented the Ada Simmons MLK Scholarship Award,

2016 Alpha Kappa Alpha South Central Regional Julia Brogdon Purnell Humanitarian Award (2nd Place), and 2019 McKinney Volunteer of the Year.

Mrs. Thelma Ree Burton Byrd
Age 99

The Interview

What advice would you give to a younger person today?

My mother taught me the following, and I want to share it with them:

- Always trust in God and let Him be your guide.
- Keep God first, always be nice to people, and remember you can't treat them alike, *but* you can treat them right.
- You will never lose in life when you put God first in whatever you do.

What is something you have overcome?

Surviving the death of five children and losing my husband of sixty-six years. I had to lean on God to make it through each one. My sole comfort was that I had done the best I could to raise them in the Lord. I also had to survive several grandchildren who all died young.

What are some lessons from your life experiences you believe will help others?

I live by the motto, "If I can help somebody along the way, then my living will not be in vain."

After accepting the Lord as my Savior and joining the church at age nine, I became active in the church. I served as an usher. Later, I became the president of the Sunshine Band (reaching out to other young people and telling them about Christ at an early age.) As an adult, I continued serving others in various positions in the church (including choir secretary, church financial secretary, kitchen committee, floral committee, and the benevolent ministries of the church.)

I also served the Grandview community by taking other people's children to school and feeding the neighborhood kids. Those adult children are now giving back to me what I gave them in various ways throughout the years.

I also worked for three white families, and although their parents are deceased, the children still call, visit, and have shown their appreciation through the years.

I was a part of the mission ministry which allowed me to help others (including younger women). We visited homebound people. We cleaned their homes when needed, as well as cooked meals while they studied their mission materials.

Please share your story or something you want others to know about you.

I was born on February 24, 1923, in Shreveport, LA to a family of twelve children. I was baptized at age nine in Dawson Pond by my dad and Pastor Martin.

I worked in my daddy's store and in the cotton fields for $0.50 an hour. I also had to milk the cows and feed the hogs every day before I went to school.

I married Joseph Lee Byrd on July 28, 1943, and we stayed married until his death in September 2006. I am the mother of ten biological children but have numerous other "adopted" children who still call, come by, send tokens of appreciation all the time.

Anyone who knows me will tell you that I've never met a stranger. I've been known to walk up to complete strangers and introduce myself and have them in full conversation before they know what is happening.

My faith in God is strong. This is the reason I've been able to continue with life after losing five children and my husband.

I am always very proud to tell someone when something good happens to one of my children. I don't try to run my adult children's lives, but I'm always there to give words of wisdom, if needed.

About Me

Mrs. Thelma R. Byrd was born in Shreveport, Louisiana, on February 24, 1923, as one of twelve children born to Daisy and Albert Burton. She was married to the late Joseph Lee Byrd on July 28, 1940, in Shreveport, LA and their union lasted for sixty-six years until her husband passed away in September 2006. She is the mother of ten children, five of whom are still living today. She is also loved by her many grandchildren, great-grandchildren, great-great-grandchildren, daughters-in-law, sons-in-law, and all her "adopted" children and extended family.

She moved to Texarkana, Texas, to take care of her older sister, who was sick at the time. Her sister eventually moved to California; however, the Byrd family remained in Texarkana. Ms. Thelma united with the St. Paul Missionary Baptist Church on Christmas morning in 1953 under Pastor B.C. Green. She sang in the church choir for over sixty years. Her community involvement over the years includes:

- Serving on the committee to hire the first black policeman in Texarkana
- After the integration of the schools, one of the first blacks from Grandview school to work with the PTA
- Served as a grandmother of the St. Paul MBC Girls Scout troop #441
- Served on the Model City Health committee which worked on getting the streets in the Grandview community paved, replacing the mud and dust which were both a health issue to citizens
- Received a community citizen's award from Hamilton AME Church
- Honored (October 2013) as the "oldest living descendent" of one of the founders (her father) of the Paige Chapel Baptist Church, Shreveport, Louisiana

She is currently ninety-nine years old and is looking forward to her 100th birthday. Mrs. Byrd says that she "Thanks the Good Lord for everything He has done in her life, and that she will keep on serving and praising Him" for the rest of her life.

Ms. Grace Rutherford
AGE 79

The Interview

What advice would you give to a younger person today?

I would advise a younger person to put God first in everything they do.

Listen to the advice when it is given and don't be quick to turn a deaf ear. We live in a time where technology and education is good, but wisdom and sound advice is necessary. Remember, seniors (older people) have traveled roads you have yet to travel. Sometimes they made poor decisions, and some could not be corrected. I have heard it said, "Why tell me not to do this when you did it?" This is the reason: if you listen to advice from someone who has experience, you can avoid making the same mistake. Perhaps that will allow the outcome for you to be different.

Never forget or be ashamed of where you come from.

Regardless of how much you accomplish in life, it's not where you started; it's where you end up. Without God, you couldn't do anything. Whatever you accomplished, He permitted it, because He moves in mysterious ways, sometimes ways we do not understand. When we take God out of the equation, things go wrong.

Always love one another and treat others the way you desire to be treated. When I say everyone, I mean just that.

Always respect the elders.

What is something you have overcome?

In May 1992, my doctor diagnosed breast cancer in my left breast. I did what I knew to do according to Isaiah 53:5: (KJV) *But he was wounded for our transgressions, he was bruised for our iniquities: the chastisement of our peace was upon him: and with his stripes we are healed.* I went through the necessary medical procedures by having a mastectomy surgery and the required rounds of chemotherapy. During the chemotherapy process, I had to have emergency surgery because a tube broke on the inside and traveled to my lungs. Thanks to God, everything went well with the surgery. After weeks of chemotherapy and the required doctor follow-up visits, they gave me a clean bill of health. Thank God for the victory! I was blessed with another good report.

Twenty years later, July 2012, I had left knee replacement. The next year, July 2013, I had a right knee replacement, and again I came out with the victory on both occasions. Thank God!

On October 15, 2015, I lost my husband. In the next month, my doctor diagnosed breast cancer in the right breast. I was confident the Lord would never leave me neither forsake me. With His help and the support of my four children, family, and Christian friends, I went through the process again. After twenty-three years, methods had changed in the way treatments were done. Within a two-year period, I was declared cancer-free once more. Thank God for the victory again!

What is your story or something you want others to know about you?

I became a single mother after eight years of marriage. I had three children, ages seven, three, and eight months, and was pregnant with number four. I loved my children and said to myself, "With the help of the Lord, I am going to take care of my children." I knew I had a journey ahead of me. I would seek the Lord daily for direction. Believe me, the journey wasn't easy at times, but the Lord always made a way. I was a licensed cosmetologist. I used the knowledge I learned in school, became a seamstress, and did typing for the churches in the community. I never turned my back on God. He said in His Word the journey would not be easy. I always remained faithful to God, to the best of my ability. There were times I know I got off the path, but we can always get back on the right path. In my senior years, I am more aware of the importance of making God top priority in my life by living according to His Word. I strive to be an example for the younger generation.

What are some lessons from your experiences you believe will help others?

Everyone is different.

It's important to listen before giving advice or making a comment.

Do not get involved in other people's affairs unless asked, but be sure they want you involved.

When transacting important business, it is very important that everything is put into writing and signed by all parties involved.

Angelia Hayes and mom Grace Rutherford

About Me

Grace Rutherford was born in a small community called "Bell Bottom" on the outside of Bay City, Texas. She was raised in a family of four children. She was the only girl. Her parents taught them three important factors for life: how to work hard and be responsible, to treat each other with love and respect, and to always carry themselves in a godly manner. She graduated from O H Herman High School in Van Vleck, Texas. Next, she attended Franklin Beauty School in Houston, Texas, where she later graduated as a licensed cosmetologist.

Shortly after becoming a cosmetologist, she put her skills to work in a local beauty shop. Grace didn't stop there but took on an entrepreneurial role in her community as a cosmetologist with her specialized service in press and curl of women and children's hair.

After becoming a wife and mother, Grace stayed home a few years and used her sewing and typing skills in the community and for local churches. She also continued to put her cosmetology skills to work in various beauty shops.

A few years later, she attended Brazosport Junior College to complete a course in Office Education. Grace is a fifteen-year retiree of Brazosport Memorial Hospital and a former home health provider. While working at the hospital, Grace developed a love for completing and filing tax returns for family and friends. She continues to demonstrate a strong work ethic with twenty-two years as a tax preparer for H&R Block. She looks forward to her twenty-third year in servicing her tax clients. Grace enjoys spending time with her family and friends and serving in her church and community.

Ms. Pat Watkins
Age 87

The Interview

What advice would you give to a younger person today?

Be true to yourself and don't try to be anyone you are not. God had a reason for creating you just the way you are.

Don't be afraid to take risks or make mistakes. Both will move the needle forward in the long run.

Be an encourager. The world needs more positive people.

"Two prisoners looked out from prison bars. One saw the mud. The other saw the stars."

~ Dale Carnegie

What is something you have overcome?

Weight issues. Up until high school, I was quite chubby. Because I cared deeply about what others thought of me, my self-esteem suffered greatly. But the biggest motivator for losing the weight was that I was an athlete, and the extra weight hindered my performance. I became more active, practiced harder, and cut out the sweets. Walking away from my mom's coconut pie about killed me! It was all worth it, though, as I excelled in sports and became a volleyball coach. The issue wasn't about being thin. It was about self-discipline and achieving my goal.

Divorce/Betrayal: Even though my husband of twenty-five years was the one who betrayed me, it was difficult for me to sop blaming myself. I lost confidence during this extremely painful time. It took a while, but Hard work brought renewed confidence and I became my own person again. In my post-divorced life (I never remarried), I found the courage to start over in a new town, learn new hobbies like golf, and turn strangers into friends. From a small town Physical Education teacher to a happy and fulfilled University professor, I achieved more on my own than I ever thought possible.

"Only those who dare to fail greatly can ever achieve greatly." ~Robert F. Kennedy

What are some lessons from your life experiences that you believe will help others?

Last year, I made the hard decision to give up my independence and move into an assisted-living facility due to some health issues. I had lived by myself for over forty years, and leaving my beloved home was excruciating. The first few months in my "new home" were pretty miserable—I had already made up my mind that I wasn't going to like living there. I made no effort to engage with my new community. I wasted valuable time feeling sorry for myself.

Then one day I made a conscious decision to change my attitude, become more involved, and open myself up to those I met. So many good friends had cared for me through the years, it was time to pay it forward. I chose to be happy, began to focus on the positive, and that has changed my quality of life.

After about nine months of living in the assisted-living facility, I was faced with the decision of selling my home. I felt that as long as I kept my house, I had the option of moving back in when I was better. Even though I was adjusting to my new life, I still viewed my current situation as temporary. After much thought and prayer, selling my home became the reasonable option. Once my mind was made up, we moved fast, and it was done. I had to burn the bridge to keep from going backward. With that came emotional relief and a newfound freedom to live a simpler life.

"Keep your face always toward the sunshine—and the shadows will fall behind you.

~Walt Whitman

Share your story or something you want others to know about you.

First and foremost, my three daughters are my biggest accomplishment in life.

I am proud of my choices, and I truly mean it when I encourage others to choose wisely. You can choose to be a victim, or an overcomer. I'm grateful to be an overcomer.

About Me

Pat Watkins is a lifelong leader and learner. Her career started as a Physical Education teacher and ended as a Professor at Texas Lutheran University. At the age of eighty-seven, Pat resides in Seguin, Texas where she has stayed active in her community, serving on several boards, attending bible studies, and volunteering regularly at the Guadalupe Regional Wellness Center. She considers her greatest accomplishment to be her three daughters— Tanya, Terri, and Paige.

~Insights and Reflections~

~Insights and Reflections~

Ms. Mary Lou Birdsong Wayne
AGE 90

The Interview

What advice would you give to a younger person today?

Never change yourself to fit in with others. Be true to yourself.

What is something you have overcome?

Over 50 years ago, the heart doctors at Cedar Sinai Hospital in Los Angeles said I needed a heart transplant. They placed me on a heart transplant list and waited year after year. The call never came. I overcame their diagnosis and allowed God to take over my mind, body, and soul. All these years, I've continued to pray, and God has been gracious to me. I'm still here.

What are some lessons from your life experiences you believe will help others?

I encouraged my children to live a good life and put God first. I also encouraged them to raise their children like I raised them. And when you have the means to help somebody, just do it!

Share your story or something you want others to know about you.

God allowed me to celebrate my 90th birthday on July 14, 2022. When I look back over my ninety years of life, I think about:

- how far I've come
- what I had to go through
- my spiritual journey
- my life as a mother
- the burial of three of my eight children
- the burial of seven brothers and one sister

I sit and shake my head sometimes, looking back from being raised in a little town named Greenwood, across the Texas state line. Number four of thirteen children. I wonder how Mama and Daddy did it. I struggled sometimes with eight children, but God's grace kept me rooted in His word and the values my parents raised me on.

I moved to Los Angeles, CA at the tender age of eighteen, married with one child. We lived with a sibling until I could get on my feet. I joined Solid Rock Baptist Church where my uncle, Rev. Sidney Birdsong, was pastor and began singing in the choir.

I worked over forty years as a custodian for the Los Angeles School System and picked up extra work wherever I could to make ends meet.

When my husband and I went our separate ways, I found myself a single mother of five boys and three girls. "Help me, Lord!" was my daily prayer to raise them in a Godly way and teach them to be true to themselves. I would tell them, "If you can't be true to yourself, how can you be true to someone else?"

I began having medical issues with my heart. The doctors at Cedars-Sinai Medical Center told me they would place me on a heart transplant list, and when a heart became available, they would notify me. To this day, that call never came. I prayed daily—and still pray—that God would continue to give me life, knowing what the prognosis was.

The doctor still tells me I have a weak heart, and I tell him my faith is stronger.

I am reminded of when Mary and Martha sent for Jesus saying, "Whom thou lovest is sick." (John 11:3-4 KJV). When Jesus heard that, He said, "This sickness is not unto death, but for the glory of God, that the Son of God might be glorified thereby." Jesus loved Mary, Martha, and Lazarus, but lingered two more days before coming to them.

I felt like those sisters. I knew God loved me, and if it was for me to have a heart transplant, then it would happen. Ninety years and I'm still here; heart not as strong as it could be, but the grace of God has kept me all these years. The doctors gave up on me, but God didn't.

I remind my children that through everything I've gone through, I did my best to raise them in a Christian home. I worked hard to do the best that I could. Be good mothers and fathers and teach your children the right way to go. Nothing wrong with tough love, my children turned out well. They take good care of me now, and I never have to want anything.

I remind them that even though I didn't have much when they were growing up, the little that I had, I tried to use to help someone else. I remind them there is someone who doesn't have what we have—no safe place to live or can't buy food for their children. If you have the means, reach out and help somebody when you see a need. "That's where your blessings come from because that's how God wants us to live."

I've outlived children, brothers, and a sister, and being the matriarch of my family at the age of ninety is a blessing. I don't know what the future holds for me, but I know *Who* holds my future. Thank you for allowing me to share my words of life, wisdom and love. May God bless all of you.

Mary Lou and Sister Ardinia

About Me

I am the jewel who was born in Greenwood, Louisiana, the fourth child of George and Ola Mae Birdsong. I married the boy next door, moved to the west coast, and became the mother of eight children. Through the years, my family has grown to twelve grandchildren, nineteen great-grands, and thirteen great-great-grands. I am a proud mother who consistently encourages my children to do well in life. They have not disappointed me. I love life itself and all it has to offer.

Coming up in a small town, opportunities were out of my reach. I desperately wanted to venture beyond the little town sitting on the Texas-Louisiana line. Indeed, I did. I never wanted to be a stay-at-home mother. I ventured into the workforce and enjoyed employment with the Los Angeles Unified School District which spanned nearly forty years. The Lord blessed me to retire. I worked hard to give my family the best life could offer.

Even though doctors told me I had a bad heart, it never slowed me down. Giving up was not on my radar. Now at ninety years old, I'm still living a fruitful life.

God is my very present help in the time of need.

Afterword
By: Venezuela Williams

I Wouldn't Change My Journey!

Maya Angelou once said, "Courage is the most important of all the virtues because, without courage, you can't practice any other virtue consistently. You can practice any virtue erratically, but nothing consistently, without courage." Courage is very similar to the idea of heroism since they both mean bravery and valor.

This describes the women who shared their stories with you in Volume I and II. This courage thing is the real cure! As we traversed Volume II of the courageous strength of these women, I am sure you are wondering, *How are they still standing after all they have been through?* Renewing their strength through courage and using the power of their voices is how they all have become the women they are today. Despite their voices being silenced for so long, one day, that courage was strong enough to stand on its own.

They realized the best thing one can do for oneself is live a fulfilling life and do all things that make you happy. In Volume I, the stories touched you at your core. They made you look within the core of who you are based on life events, both challenging and rewarding. I can imagine most of you who read this book can see yourself in the various situations of each story shared. Which story resonated with you? How can you use your courage to settle past wounds?

The stories also transformed you from living with pain to living with healing, to find your purpose. They shared their most vulnerable states of mind, body, and soul. The women in Volume II lifted your spirits as they shared their most intimate thoughts and experiences. As you can see, dealing with your past pain can help you heal and tear down your "unhealable" state of mind. In fact, you saw how their purpose was birthed from that healing.

Are you looking to live a new life free of your past? I hope so! We all have a story to tell that will change others' lives, so as you read each story, one by one, I am quite sure you could see yourself, a friend, a family member, or even a coworker in her shoes. It is okay to share your experiences and how you have overcome that hurt, disappointment, or loss of hope. It is who you are and what has made you the woman you are today. Remember, ladies, a bottle of water can be fifty cents at a grocery store, two dollars at the gym, three dollars at the movie theater, and six dollars on the airplane. Yes, the water is the same. The only thing that changed its value was the location. So, hear this: the next time you feel your worth is nothing, maybe you are in the wrong location, with the wrong person, or investing in the wrong thing. You, too, can overcome all the upheavals of your past. So, celebrate that past, embrace the future, and seek that authentic side of you! I promise there is a way. Get that VICTORY as you are a WINNER!

"'For I know the plans I have for you' declares the Lord, 'plans to prosper you and not to harm you, plans to give you hope and a future.'"

Venezuela Williams, best-selling author, Human Resources and Business professional. I am here to serve you! For more guidance, one-on-one personal coaching sessions, motivational speaker, or moderator, reach out to me via IG: Venezuela_vault or venezuelawilliams.com.

Phyllis Byrd Jenkins

Telling Our Stories anthology, Founder
Phyllis Byrd Jenkins

Christ follower, purpose-driven, visionary, passion and perseverance are core values of Phyllis.

She's a certified professional coach, author, international speaker, founder of the Powerful Journey Organization, and host of the PowerLift Stories podcast. Thousands of lives have been impacted through the Powerful Journey platforms: Author's Academy, Telling Our Stories anthology, Speaker's Academy, The Water-Walking Masterclass, and our signature event, the annual Powerful Journey Women's Conference.

Phyllis helps women tell their stories, write their books, and build a profitable brand around both. The Water-Walking Masterclass helps high achievers launch, expand, and scale their businesses. The Voyage Dallas Magazine featured Phyllis, she was winner of the Think and Grow Rich Eagle Award with Dan Miller, winner of the Doreen Rainey "My Business is Radical" contest, and recipient of the Plano Community Forum Civic Award. Phyllis gives back to the community by awarding scholarships to single moms of special needs children (the Madian Chumbley Scholarship) and by awarding the Mildred Ida Byrd Pugh Scholarship to a graduating high school senior. She is a member of the Alpha Kappa Alpha Sorority, Inc., and a graduate of Amberton University. Phyllis is married to her college sweetheart, Dave, and has two adult daughters and three amazing grandchildren.

Phyllis believes everyone has overcome something. Regardless of age or life-stage. That means everyone has a story. She is soaring in her sixties as she helps women (and a few men) turn their life challenges into life-changing messages. Messages of hope, inspiration, and encouragement that will help others not only survive, but THRIVE.

It's TIME for YOU to Tell Your Story and write your book! I invite you to join one of the Powerful Journey Platforms.

Author's Academy

Telling Our Stories Anthology

PowerLift Stories Podcast

Your Significant Story Workshop: Turn Your Life Challenges into Life-Changing Messages

Sign up for the Powerful Journey Newsletters

Launching December 2022—Powerful Journey Writers Membership Program

Annual Powerful Journey Women's Conference (In-Person or Virtual)

www.phyllisjenkins.com   www.tellingourstories.info

email: Phyllis@phyllisjenkins.com

Dear Reader,

This Anthology of Faith is a testament to the faithfulness of God.

If you do not know Jesus as your Savior and Lord, simply pray this prayer in faith, and Jesus will be your Lord!

Dear Lord Jesus, I know I am a sinner, and I ask for Your forgiveness. I believe You died for my sins and rose from the dead. I turn from my sins and invite You to come into my heart and life. I want to trust and follow You as my Lord and Savior. Amen.

After you pray this prayer, please connect with me so I can CELEBRATE with you!

The *Telling Our Stories* anthology, volume I, sold 1001 copies in just sixteen days and made the #1 New Release in Religious Arts & Photography on Amazon. With over 3,000 copies sold to date, this book is full of brave women who emerged as champions from tough situations.

Use the QR code to order your copy from Amazon today.

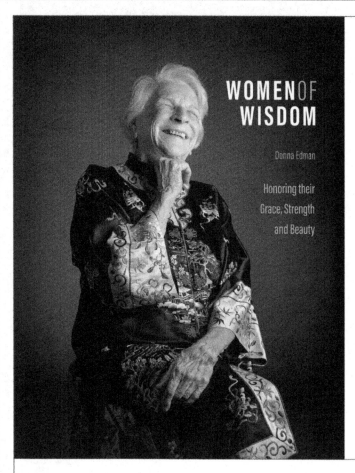

Angelia Hayes

Organization/Business: Unique Foundations Enterprise, LLC

Address: 209 Laurie Ln. Angleton, TX 77515
Phone: 979-334-2648
Email: uniquefoundations@icloud

Dave Jenkins
COACHING
Life Coach | Marriage Coach

Has Communicating become a challenge in your marriage? I Help Couples "Transform Relationship Breakdowns Into Relationship Breakthroughs ™"

Dave Jenkins – Certified Marriage and Life Coach

How would it feel to have a loving, supportive, and healthy marriage?

To schedule a free coaching session, go to the link below.
https://davejenkinscoaching.setmore.com
Or email me at dave@davejenkinscoaching.com.
Text RELATIONSHIP to 833-246-9944 to get your free marriage resource.

Reconnect – Recommit—Rekindle Your Relationship

JACKIE CASTLE
AUTHOR

Jackie J. R. Castle writes inspirational fantasy and romance stories straight from the heart. Visit Castle's Story World. One never knows what new adventure awaits them around the next corner.

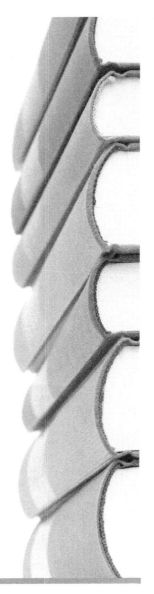

Castle Book Creations' goal is to help fellow authors with their publishing needs. We aim to help authors give their stories professional covers and presentations at a reasonable price. Visit Castle's Story World to learn more.
Mention POWERFUL WOMEN for a 20% discount on your next book cover.

CASTLE
BOOK COVERS

WWW.JACKIECASTLE.COM

Made in the USA
Las Vegas, NV
08 October 2022

56797173R20057